Counting and Recognition to Five

Written by Sue Lambert and Sandi Rickerby

Published by World Teachers Press®

Order Number 2-5100
ISBN 1-58324-022-5

A B C D E F 03 02 01 00 99

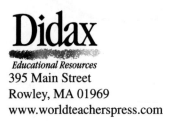

Educational Resources
395 Main Street
Rowley, MA 01969
www.worldteacherspress.com

Foreword

The *Early Skills Series* of books is designed to give students practice in a range of early reading, writing and number activities as well as to develop perceptual and fine motor skills in the early years.

Early Skills Series – Counting and Recognition to Five contains activities enabling students to recognize and practice tracing, writing and counting numerals one to five.

The worksheets can be used to motivate students to work independently, increase their concentration span and develop their ability to work in an orderly fashion, encouraging them to take pride in the presentation of their work at the same time.

The worksheets are bold, uncluttered and visually appealing to young students. They contain instructions in visual form, thereby requiring minimum support from you. They can be used to teach a new skill or to reinforce and consolidate those already taught.

Other books in this series are:

Early Skills Series – Early Visual Skills
Early Skills Series – Addition to Five
Early Skills Series – Cutting Activities

Contents

Teacher Information

Introduction

Development of perceptual and fine motor skills in the early years is extremely important if students are to have a good grounding to progress to the next level of development. The *Early Skills Series* is designed to provide practice in the aforementioned areas in a range of early reading, writing and math areas of the curriculum.

The worksheets are motivational and designed to encourage students to work independently wherever possible. This encourages high self-esteem, increases the student's concentration span and develops the ability to work in a logical and orderly fashion.

The clear layout of each worksheet allows the student to concentrate solely on the task at hand. The large, open artwork appeals to students and has been drawn at the appropriate level for the students' fine motor skill development.

Suggested Implementation

The *Early Skill Series* can be implemented easily into any existing program.

1. Familiarize students with the icons on pages 6 and 7. These pages could be enlarged, colored and displayed in a prominent position within the classroom. Students can then refer to the icons whenever they need to.

2. Develop recognition and understanding of the key words shown on the worksheets. Students may learn to read these words as sight words. This will help with their independence in completing the worksheets.

3. Discuss and explain each worksheet after all students have their worksheets in front of them.

   (a) Students sit on the mat area. You have an enlarged version of the worksheet.
   (b) Discuss the icons at the top of the worksheet. Students can offer you instructions for the page.
   (c) Work through the page, showing the students the completed product.
   (d) Students move back to their own area to complete the worksheet independently.

4. Worksheets can be collected and viewed to determine areas of need for each student or the whole class group.

Teachers Notes

Instructions

The instructions provided on each worksheet are in graphic form, thereby requiring minimum support from the teacher. A key explaining each graphic is located on pages 6 and 7.

Benefits

The benefits of the *Early Skills Series* are many.

1. You can readily evaluate where each student is having success or difficulties.
2. Students are provided with the opportunity to work independently.
3. Students develop perpetual and fine motor skills in the areas of early reading, writing and numbers..
4. Students become familiar with a general range of instructional text.
5. Students are able to develop logic and work in an orderly fashion.
6. The worksheets are highly motivational.
7. The program is easy to implement into any classroom.
8. Many coloring activities are left as open ended to help develop creative and decision making skills.

Conclusion

The Early Skills Series provides worksheets to cover *Early Visual Skills, Cutting, Counting and Recognition to Five* and *Addition to Five*; areas which are of major significance in the students' development in the early years of education. A solid grounding in these areas ensures smooth progression onto the next level of development. The activities are designed to allow the students to experience success, developing confidence and a positive self-image towards themselves as a learner.

Key-Counting and Recognition to Five

write

Trace over or write the number.

draw

Trace over or draw the picture.

color

Color the pictures as shown.

cut

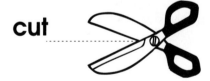

Cut along the dotted lines.

connect

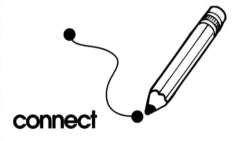

Join with a line.

Key-Counting and Recognition to Five

count

Count the pictures or numbers.

glue

Glue the pictures in the correct place.

order

Order the pictures from smallest to biggest.

Be creative.

Choose a color.

1. write

2. color

1

Name: _____ Date: _____

1. ✏️ write   2. ▭ color

2

1. ↷
2. →

2   2 2 2 2

2 2 2 2 2

2 2 2 2 2

Name: _____ Date: _____

1. ✏️ write   2. ▭ color

3

3

1 ↪ 2 ↩

3   3   3   3

3   3   3   3

3   3   3

Early Skills Series – *Counting and Recognition to Five*   World Teachers Press®

1. ✏️ write   2. ✏️ color

4

4   ↓1 →2 ↓3   4 4 4   4 4   4

4 4 4 4 4 4 4

4 4 4 4 4 4 4

1. write

2. color

5

3 →

1 ↓ 2

5

Early Skills Series – *Counting and Recognition to Five* World Teachers Press®

Name: _____ Date: _____

I. ✏️ write

1 | | |

2 2 2

3 3 3

4 4 4

5 5 5

1 2 3 4 5

Name: _____   Date: _____

1. write

2. color

1

2

3

4

5

1 2 3 4 5

Name: _____   Date: _____

1. ✏️ write   2. 🖍️ color

1

2

3

4

5

 1. count   2. color   3. cut     4. order   5. glue

Choose the Colors!
- 1 spot –
- 2 spots –
- 3 spots –
- 4 spots –
- 5 spots –

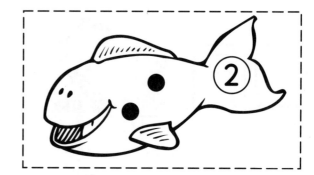

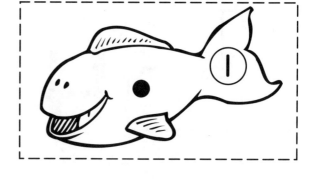

Name: _____   Date: _____

 1.   ● 2.   3. _cut_   4. ∘○◯ 5.
count   color   order   glue

Choose the Colors!

1 spot –	✏
2 spots –	✏
3 spots –	✏
4 spots –	✏
5 spots –	✏

1. color ⟨fin⟩ – orange   0 – red   2. count

Name: _____ Date: _____

1. ✏️ draw   2. 🖍 color

3

5

1

4

5

2

1.   draw   2.   color

5

1

4

2

3

4

1. count

2. connect

3. color

1

2

3

4

5

1. count   2. connect   3. color

1

2

3

4

5

1. count 2. write 3. color

	4

Name: _____ Date: _____

1. count   2. write   3. color

1. count

2. write

3. color

3

Name: _____ Date: _____

1. draw   2. color

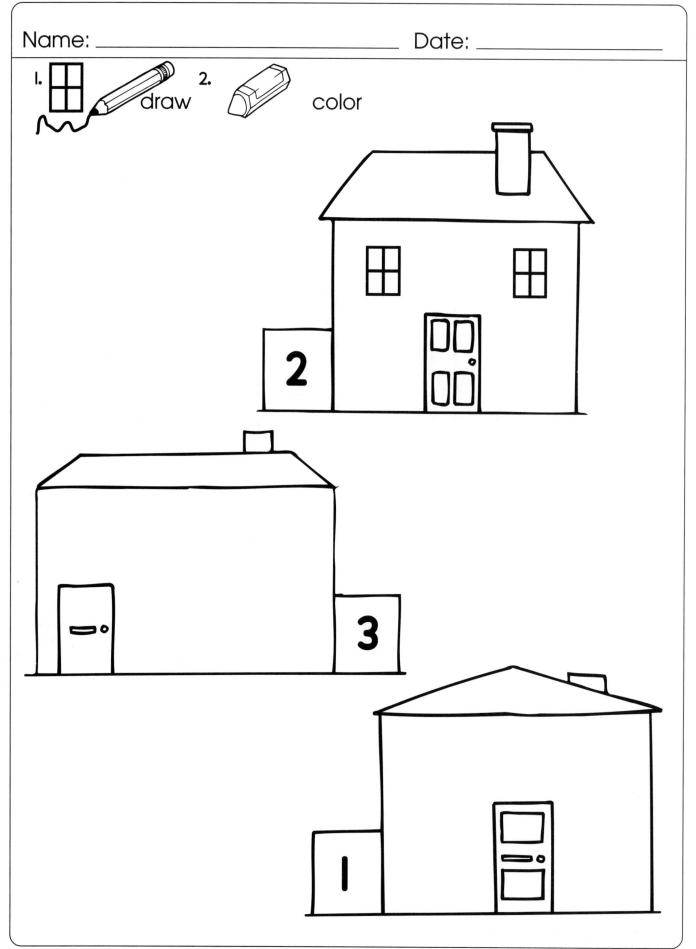

1. draw

2. color

2

4

1

3

5

1. draw

2. color

2

3

1

5

Early Skills Series – *Counting and Recognition to Five*
World Teachers Press®

Name: _____ Date: _____

1. ✏️ ⬜ draw   2. ▱ color

4

2

3

1

5

2

1. draw

2. color

5

4

3

1

2

1. count   2. write   3. color

2

Name: _____ Date: _____

1. count   2. write   3. color

Early Skills Series – *Counting and Recognition to Five*   World Teachers Press®

Name: _____ Date: _____

1. count

2. write

3. color

2

Name: _____ Date: _____

1. count   2. write   3. color

= **3**

=

=

=

=

=

Early Skills Series – *Counting and Recognition to Five*   *World Teachers Press*®

1. count   2. write   3. color

						=	

1. count

2. color

3

2

1

5

4

2

1

3

1.   count   2.   color

4   ■ ■ ■ □ □

3   ○ ○ ○ ○ ○

5   △ △ △ △ △

2   ▢ ▢ ▢ ▢ ▢

1   ◖ ◖ ◖ ◖ ◖

1   □ □ □ □ □

4   ○ ○ ○ ○ ○

2   △ △ △ △ △

1. count   2. color

4 ◯ ◯ ◯ ◯ ◯

3 △ △ △ △ △

5 ⬡ ⬡ ⬡ ⬡ ⬡

2 ⬠ ⬠ ⬠ ⬠ ⬠

1 ✦ ✦ ✦ ✦ ✦

1 ◯ ◯ ◯ ◯ ◯

4 ★ ★ ★ ★ ★

1. count

2. color

3 ○ ○ ○ ○ ○

5 △ △ △ △ △

1 ⬡ ⬡ ⬡ ⬡ ⬡

4 ⬠ ⬠ ⬠ ⬠ ⬠

2 ✦ ✦ ✦ ✦ ✦

5 ○ ○ ○ ○ ○

3 ★ ★ ★ ★ ★

Name: _____ Date: _____

1. count   2. write   3. color

5
4
3
2
1

4

3

5

Early Skills Series – *Counting and Recognition to Five*   *World Teachers Press®*

1. count   2. write   3. color

1 ___ ___ 3 ___

___ 2 ___ ___ 5

___ ___ ___ 4 ___

___ ___ ___ ___ 5

1. color

Choose the Colors!

1 —
2 —
3 —
4 —
5 —

5

4

2

1   3

5

2

1

3

I. color

Choose the Colors!
1 –
2 –
3 –
4 –
5 –

3

1

2

5

4

4

1

2

5

3

5

4

2

4

3

1

Name: _____ Date: _____

1.

color

Choose the Colors!

1 —
2 —
3 —
4 —
5 —

2

5

5

2

1

2

5

1

2

2

5

3 3 3 3 3 3

4 4 4 4 4 4 4

3 3 3 3 3 3

4 4 4 4 4 4 4

I.

color

Choose the Colors!

1 —
2 —
3 —
4 —
5 —

3 5
4
2 2
1

2 2
1 2
2 2

4 4
4 2 4
4
4

5

5 5

5

5 5

5

5

1

1

Name: _____ Date: _____

1.

color

Choose the Colors!

1 – ✏️
2 – ✏️
3 – ✏️
4 – ✏️
5 – ✏️

Name: _____ Date: _____

A sample page from the book, *Early Visual Skills*, also in the *Early Skills Series*.

1. ✏️ draw   **2.** 🖍️ color

A sample page from the book, *Cutting Activities*, also in the *Early Skills Series*.

1. color   **2.** cut ✂   **3.** glue